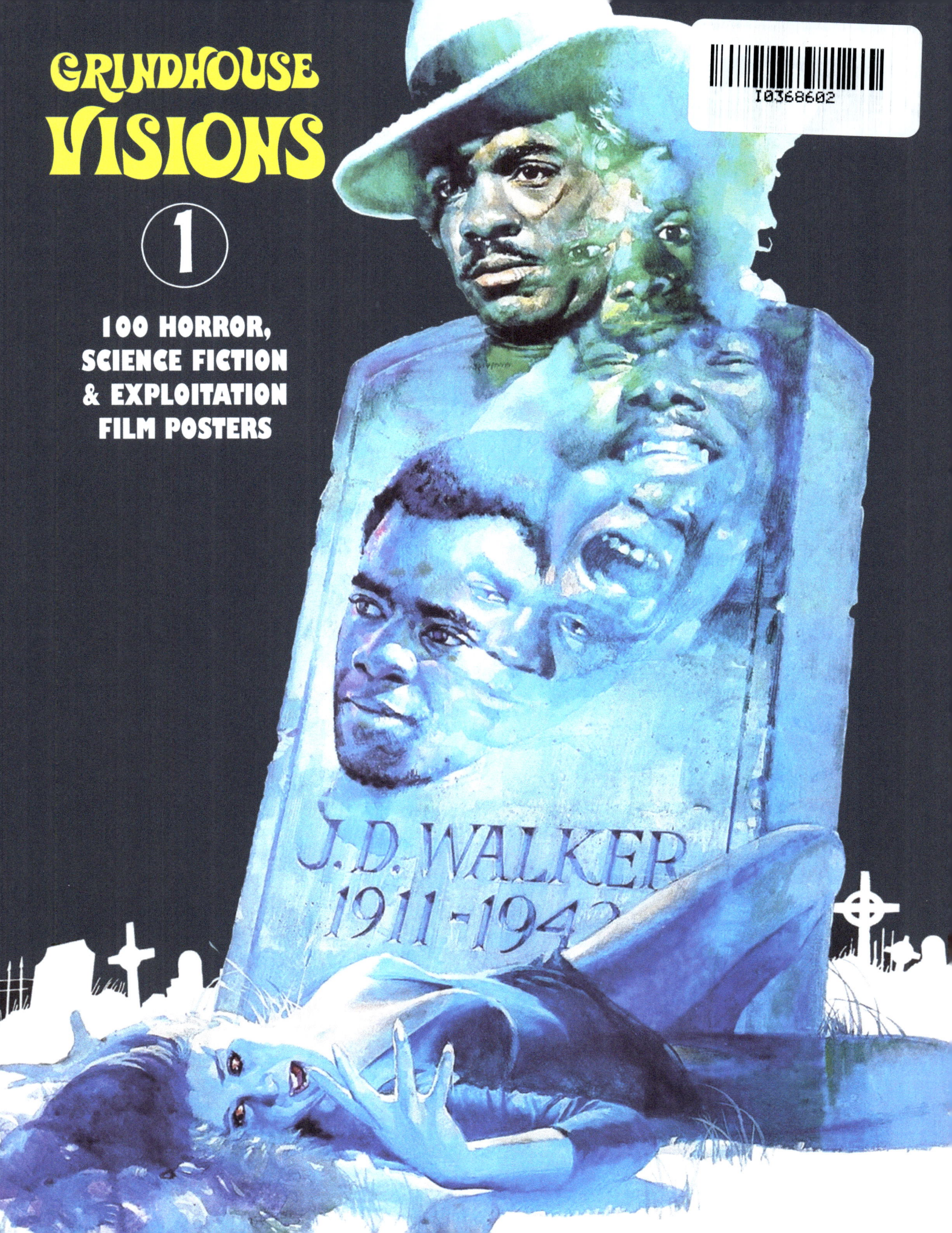

# GRINDHOUSE VISIONS

## ①

### 100 HORROR, SCIENCE FICTION & EXPLOITATION FILM POSTERS

## CONTENTS

| | |
|---|---|
| THE HOT BOX (1972) | 4 |
| THE BIG BIRD CAGE (1972) | 5 |
| THE CAULDRON OF DEATH (1979) | 6 |
| THE NAKED ROAD (1959) | 7 |
| CRY BABY KILLER (1958) | 8 |
| BIG BAD MAMA (1974) | 9 |
| THE BLACK GESTAPO (1975) | 10 |
| THE CANDY TANGERINE MAN (1975) | 11 |
| THE ZODIAC KILLER (1971) | 12 |
| THE TOWN THAT DREADED SUNDOWN (1976) | 13 |
| SWEET SUGAR (1972) | 14 |
| BORN LOSERS (1967) | 15 |
| THE HARD RIDE (1971) | 16 |
| CHROME AND HOT LEATHER (1971) | 17 |
| SADISMO (1967) | 18 |
| MONDO MOD (1967) | 19 |
| TABOOS OF THE WORLD (1963) | 20 |
| MACABRO (1966) | 20 |
| JOURNEY INTO THE BEYOND (1975) | 21 |
| MAU-MAU (1955) | 22 |
| VOODOO VILLAGE (1958) | 23 |
| VOODOO WOMAN (1957) | 24 |
| THE DISEMBODIED (1957) | 25 |
| ATTACK OF THE JUNGLE WOMEN (1959) | 26 |
| THE DEVIL'S HAND (1961) | 27 |
| BLACK SABBATH (1963) | 28 |
| FEAR CHAMBER (1968) | 29 |
| BRIDE OF THE MONSTER (1955) | 30 |
| CITY OF THE DEAD (1960) | 31 |
| THE HEADLESS GHOST (1959) | 32 |
| I WAS A TEENAGE FRANKENSTEIN (1957) | 33 |
| BLOOD BATH (1966) | 34 |
| GARDEN OF THE DEAD (1972) | 35 |
| MAN BEAST (1956) | 36 |
| MONSTER ON THE CAMPUS (1958) | 37 |
| BLOOD AND LACE (1971) | 38 |
| HORROR OF SNAPE ISLAND (1972) | 39 |
| BLACULA (1972) | 40 |
| BLOOD FROM THE MUMMY'S TOMB (1971) | 41 |
| THE CAT GIRL (1957) | 42 |
| THE HANGING WOMAN (1973) | 43 |
| THE DEVIL'S MISTRESS (1965) | 44 |
| CORPSE EATERS (1974) | 45 |
| THE DUNWICH HORROR (1970) | 46 |
| SQUIRM (1976) | 47 |
| FRANKENSTEIN AND THE MONSTER FROM HELL (1974) | 48 |
| THE VELVET VAMPIRE (1971) | 49 |
| ATOM AGE VAMPIRE (1960) | 50 |
| THE WEREWOLF (1956) | 51 |
| THE SCREAMING SKULL (1958) | 52 |
| NIGHT OF THE BLOOD BEAST (1958) | 53 |
| THE FALL OF THE HOUSE OF USHER (1960) | 54 |
| THE WITCH WHO CAME FROM THE SEA (1976) | 55 |
| MANIAC (1980) | 56 |
| THE BURNING (1981) | 57 |
| THE COOL AND THE CRAZY (1958) | 58 |
| THE BEATNIKS (1960) | 59 |
| DRAGSTRIP RIOT (1958) | 60 |
| HOT CAR GIRL (1958) | 61 |
| REFORM SCHOOL GIRL (1957) | 62 |
| RUNNING WILD (1955) | 63 |
| MOTORCYCLE GANG (1957) | 64 |
| WILD YOUTH (1960) | 65 |
| HIGH SCHOOL HELLCATS (1958) | 66 |
| UNTAMED YOUTH (1957) | 67 |
| THE ASTOUNDING SHE MONSTER (1957) | 68 |
| ATTACK OF THE 50 FT. WOMAN (1958) | 69 |
| THE BEAST WITH 1,000,000 EYES! (1955) | 70 |
| THE BRAIN EATERS (1958) | 71 |
| CYBORG 2087 (1966) | 72 |
| FIVE MILLION YEARS TO EARTH (1967) | 73 |
| GORGO (1961) | 74 |
| REPTILICUS (1961) | 75 |
| HALF HUMAN (1958) | 76 |
| QUEEN OF BLOOD (1966) | 77 |
| WAR OF THE COLOSSAL BEAST (1958) | 78 |
| TARANTULA! (1955) | 79 |
| RETURN OF THE FLY (1959) | 80 |
| THE SHE-CREATURE (1956) | 81 |
| THE TIME MACHINE (1960) | 82 |
| "X" THE MAN WITH THE X-RAY EYES (1963) | 83 |
| THE UNEARTHLY (1957) | 84 |
| VIKING WOMEN AND THE SEA SERPENT (1957) | 85 |
| BAYOU (1957) | 86 |
| THE UNSATISFIED (1961) | 87 |
| LASH OF LUST (1972) | 88 |
| BRAND OF SHAME (1968) | 89 |
| THE DEFILERS (1965) | 90 |
| LOVE CAMP 7 (1969) | 91 |
| THE FEMALE BUNCH (1971) | 92 |
| THE HITCHHIKERS (1972) | 93 |
| LIKE IT IS (1968) | 94 |
| THE TRIP (1967) | 95 |
| SPACE THING (1968) | 96 |
| THE JOYS OF JEZEBEL (1970) | 97 |
| THE ADULT VERSION OF JEKYLL AND HYDE (1972) | 98 |
| STARLET! (1969) | 99 |
| GIRLS FOR RENT (1974) | 100 |
| SCHOOLGIRLS IN CHAINS (1973) | 101 |
| ABDUCTION (1975) | 102 |
| GINGER (1971) | 103 |

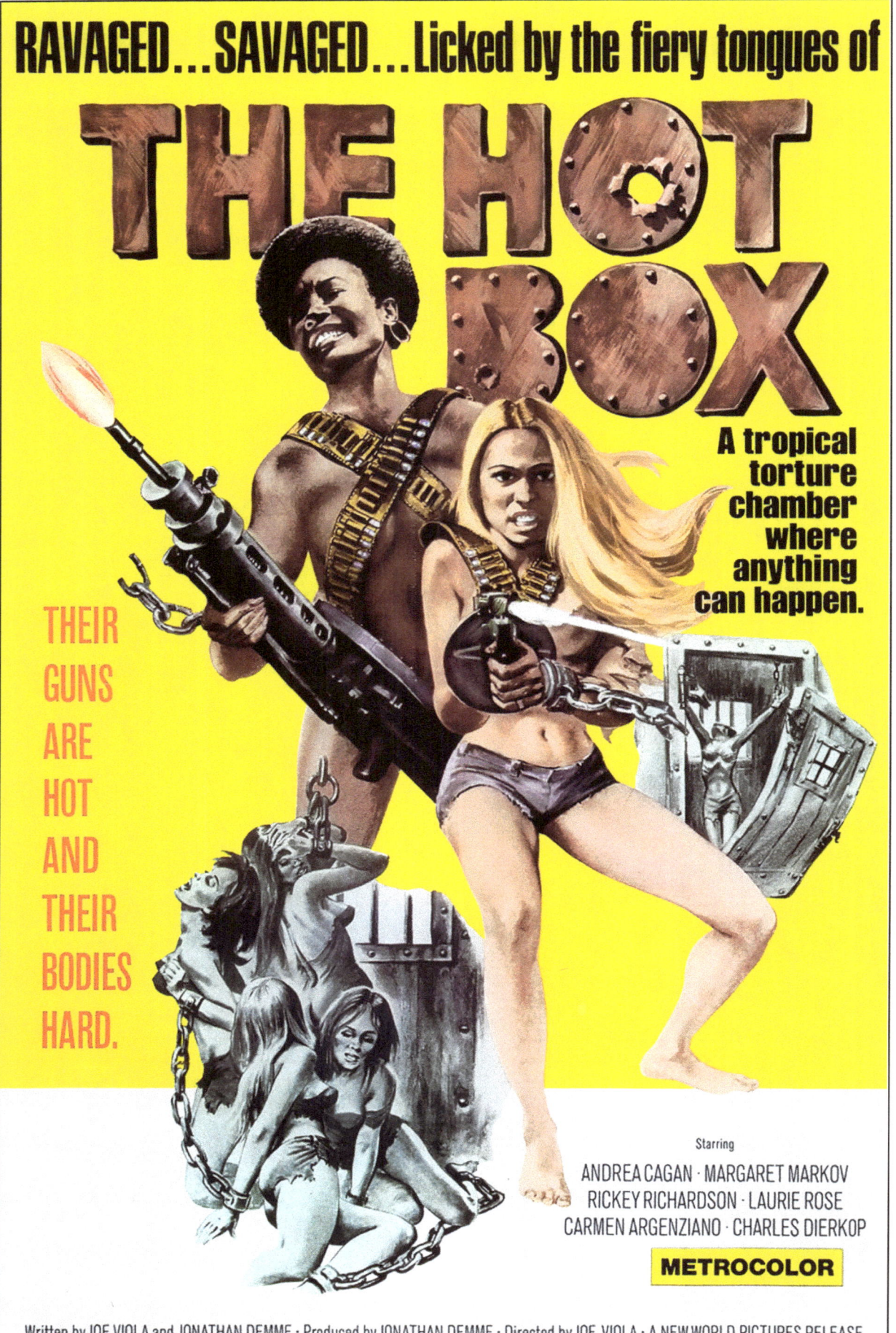

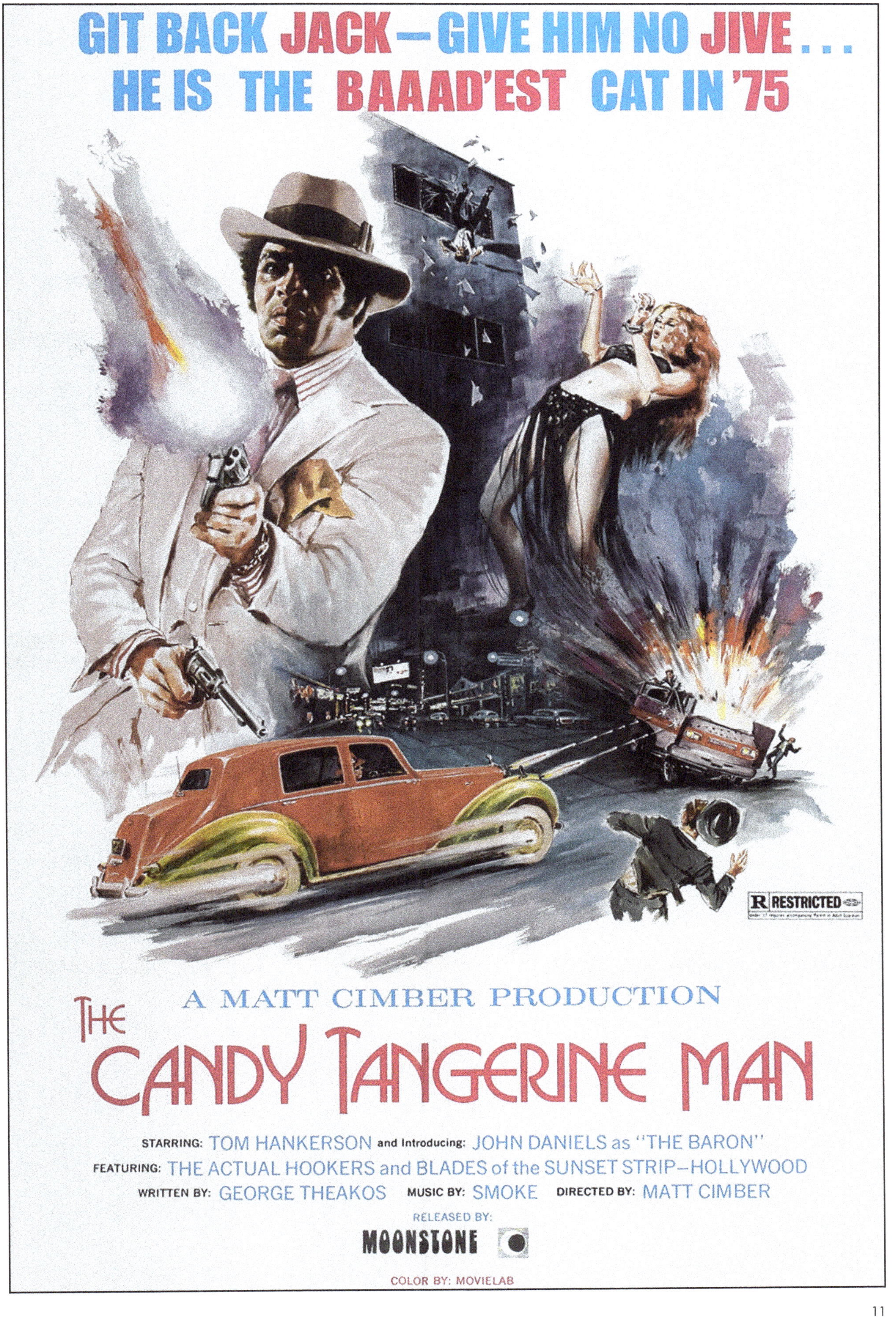
GIT BACK JACK—GIVE HIM NO JIVE . . .
HE IS THE BAAAD'EST CAT IN '75
RESTRICTED
A MATT CIMBER PRODUCTION
THE CANDY TANGERINE MAN
STARRING: TOM HANKERSON and Introducing: JOHN DANIELS as "THE BARON"
FEATURING: THE ACTUAL HOOKERS and BLADES of the SUNSET STRIP—HOLLYWOOD
WRITTEN BY: GEORGE THEAKOS MUSIC BY: SMOKE DIRECTED BY: MATT CIMBER
RELEASED BY:
MOONSTONE
COLOR BY: MOVIELAB

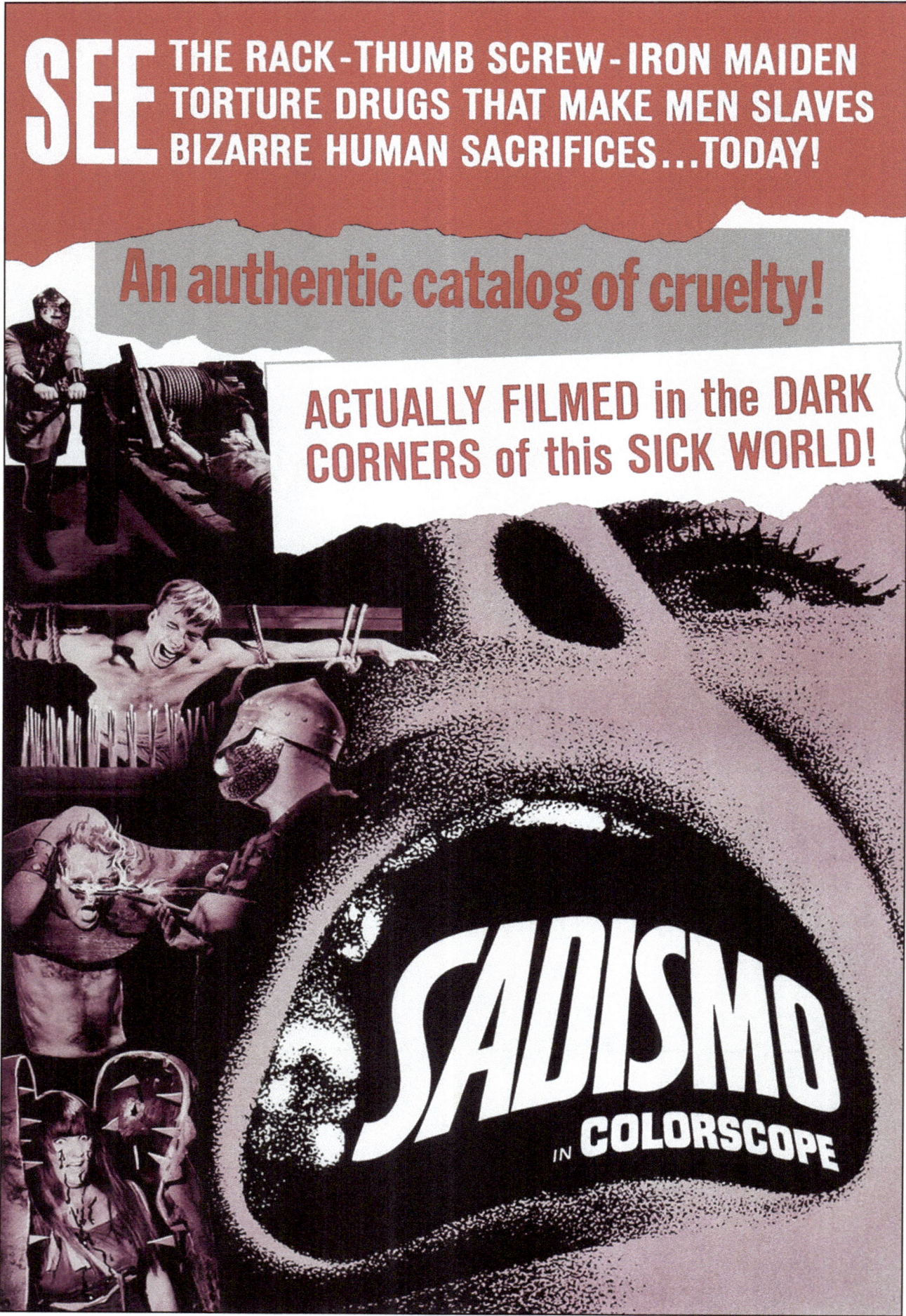

It's the film that starts where the other MONDO pictures chickened out!
AMERICAN INTERNATIONAL presents in COLOR
TABOOS
OF THE WORLD
With comments by VINCENT PRICE
Directed by ROMOLO MARCELLINI · Produced by GUIDO GIAMBARTOLOMEI

HAVE YOU THE COURAGE TO SEE THE WORLD in the RAW?
SEE EXECUTION BY PYTHON...SHOCKING WAYS OF ORIENTAL MASSAGE...
MALE GEISHA GIRLS AND THEIR STRANGE CUSTOMS...SAVAGE AFRICAN BATHING BEAUTIES...
PLAYING RUSSIAN ROULETTE WITH DIESEL TRAINS...TATTOOED VIRGINS...NAKED FISHERWOMEN OF JAPAN...
PRIMITIVE BIRTH CONTROL..."BEAUTY" EXERCISES OF SWEDISH WOMEN...EXOTIC AFRICAN LOVE SCHOOL...
SCHOOL FOR BEGGARS, WHERE CHILDREN ARE TRANSFORMED INTO MONSTERS...ANT TORTURE OF THE MAKARE
TRANS AMERICAN FILMS Presents
"MACABRO"
IN TECHNICOLOR®
...SECRETS OF THE FORBIDDEN WORLD REVEALED BY THE HIDDEN CAMERA
NARRATED BY MARVIN MILLER · PRINCIPAL DIRECTION BY ROMOLO MARCELLINI · RELEASED BY TRANS AMERICAN FILMS
66/251

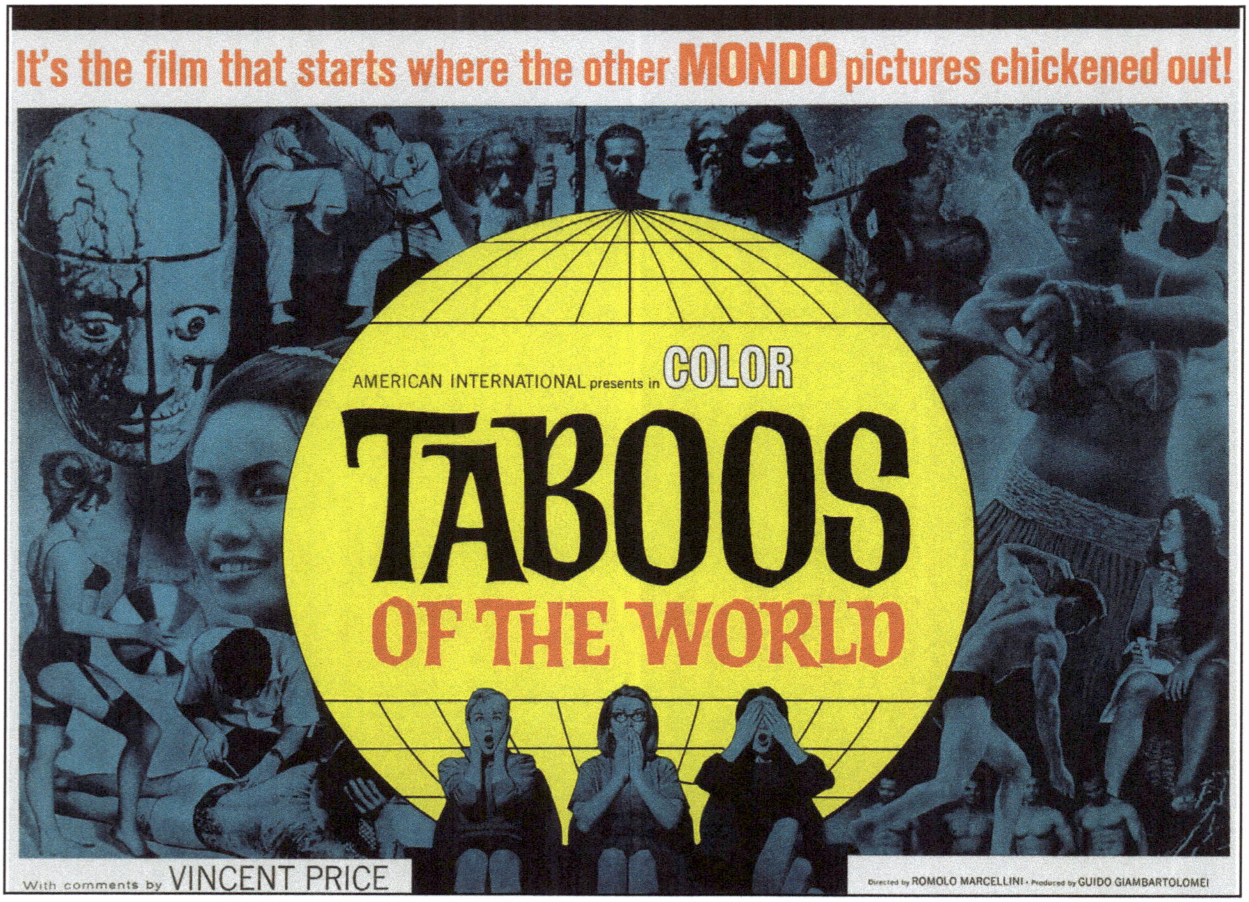

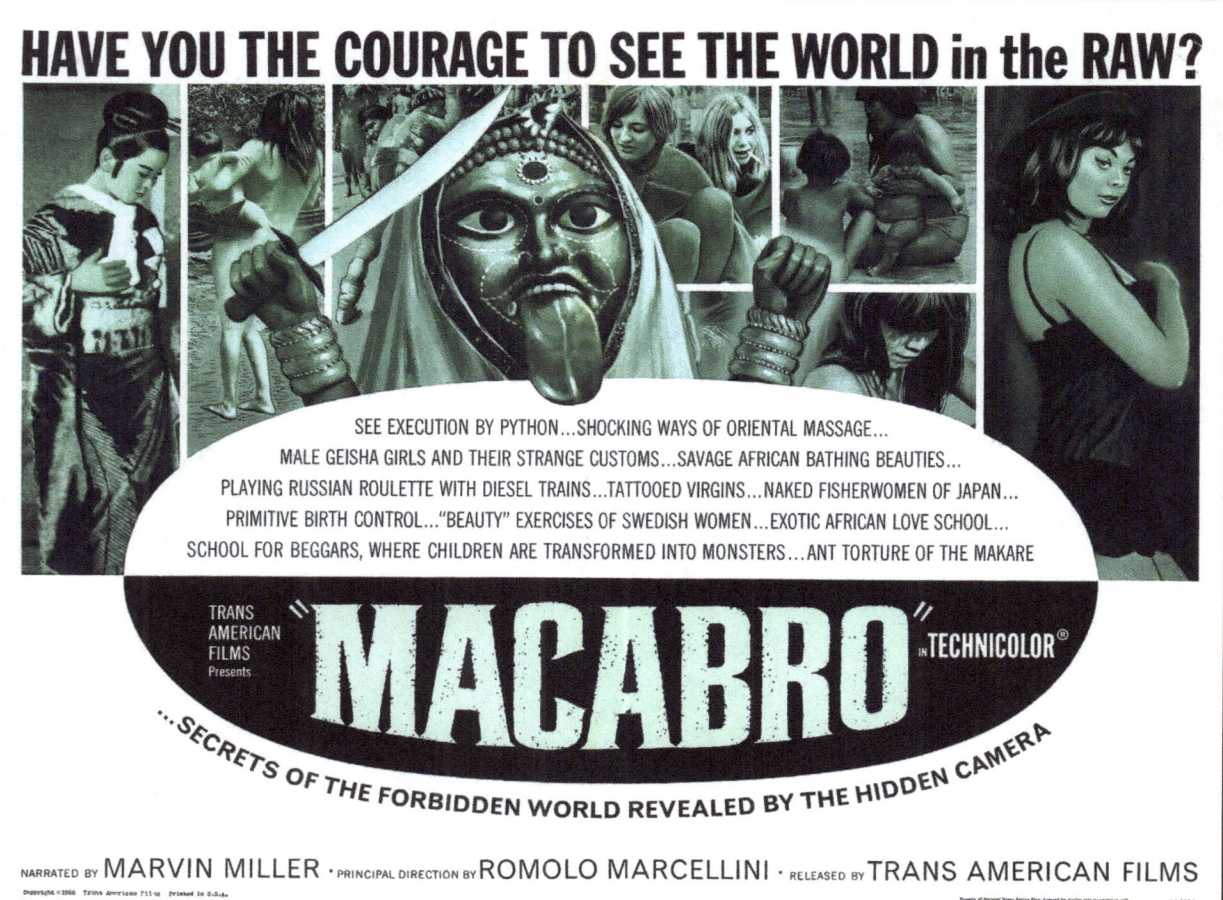

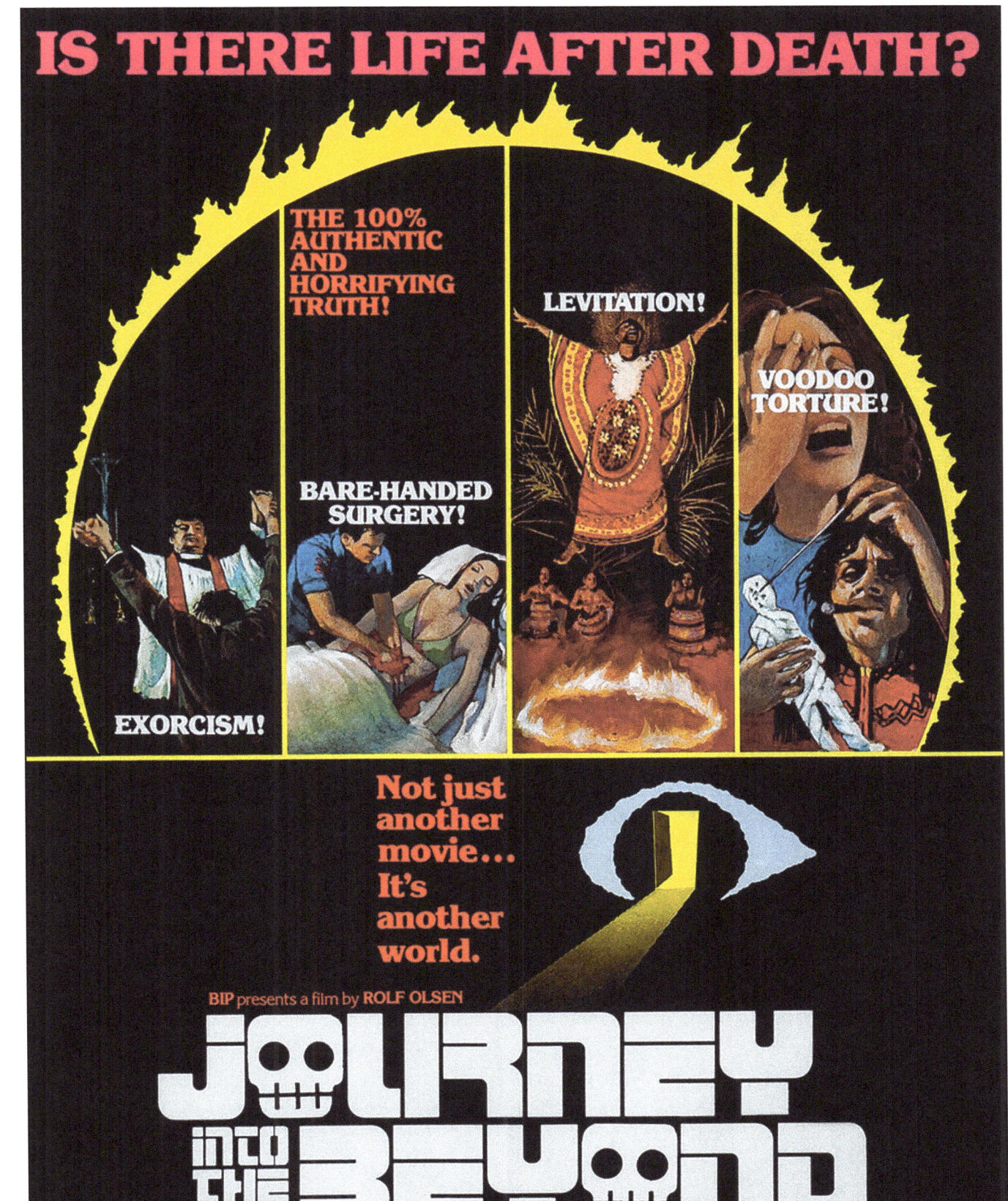

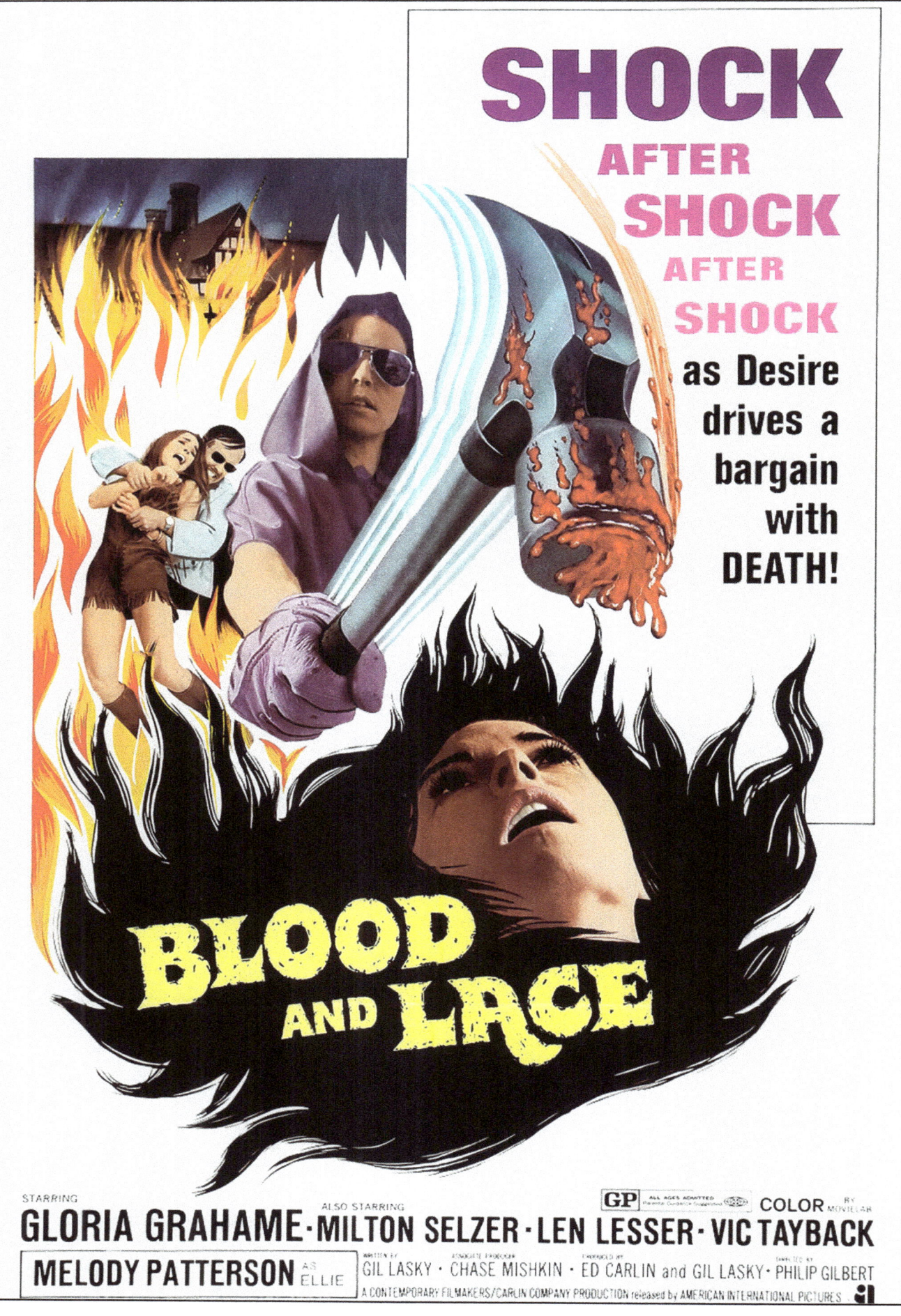

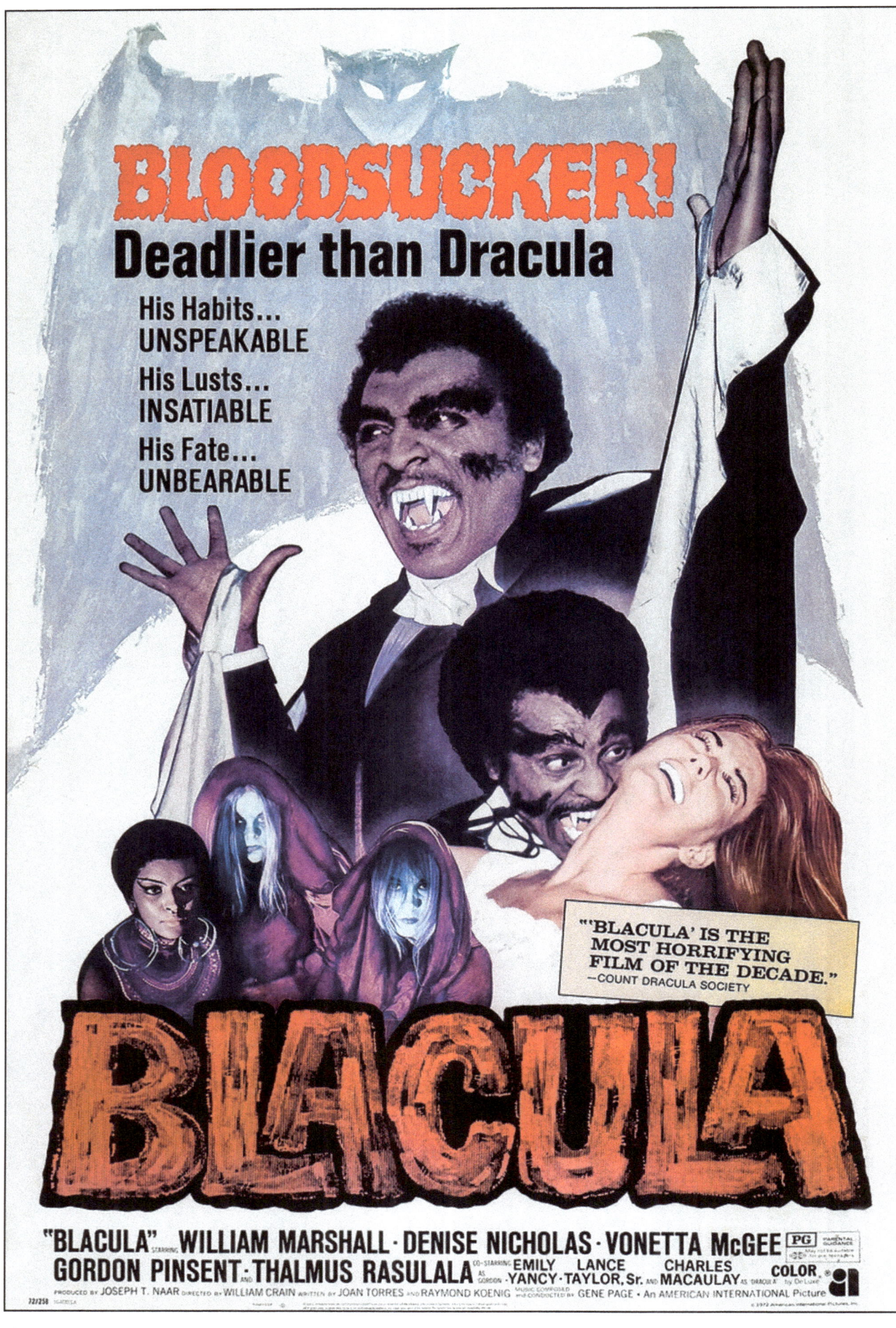

THE DEAD COME BACK-
THEY HAVE AN
UN-NATURAL HUNGER...
HUMAN BODIES!
YOU WILL BE WARNED OF SCENES THAT COULD INITIATE
INTENSE SHOCK
DURING THIS FILM!
CORPSE
EATERS
Distributed by HOWARD MAHLER FILMS, INC. COLOR BY TECHNICOLOR
R RESTRICTED

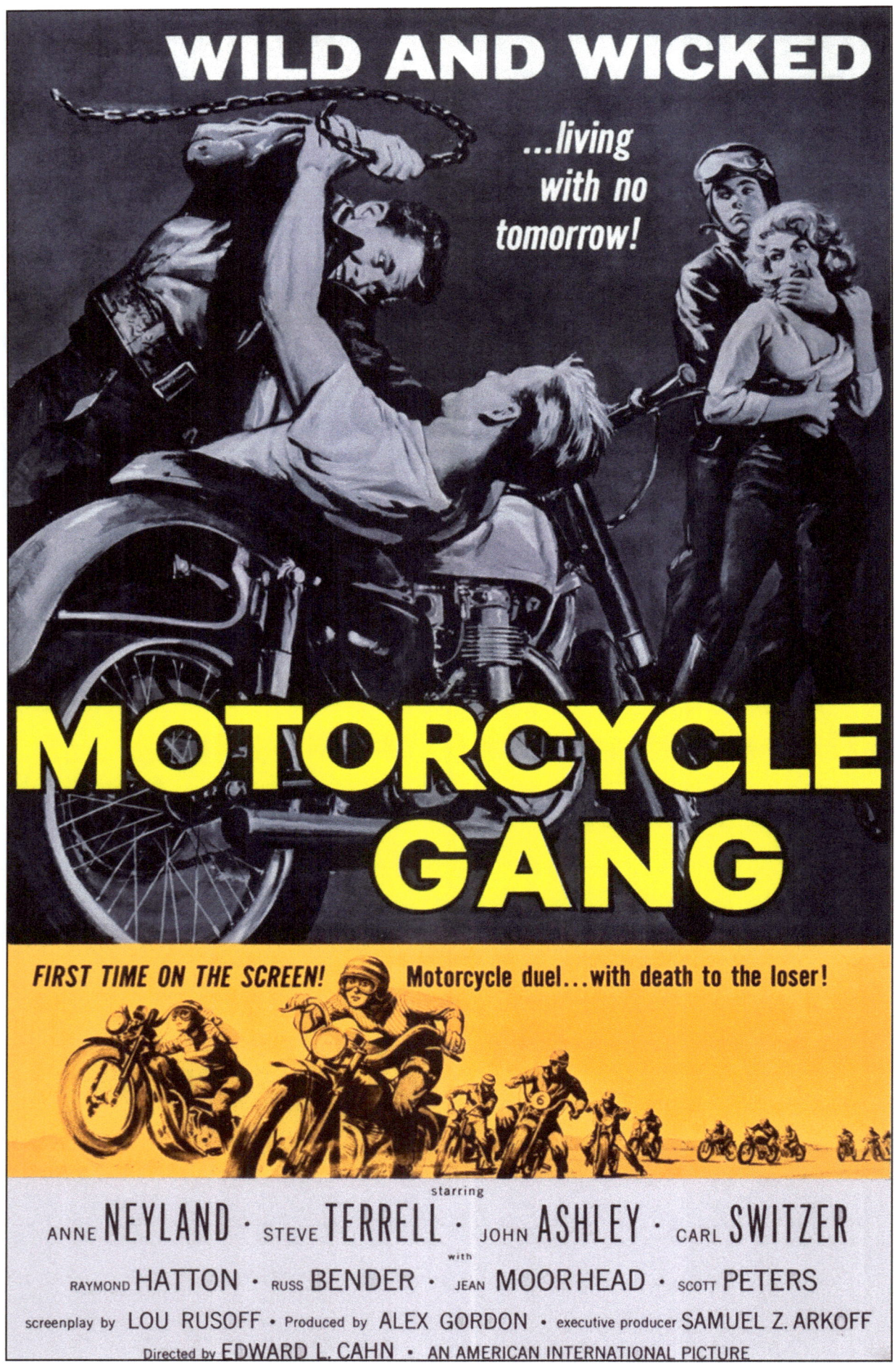

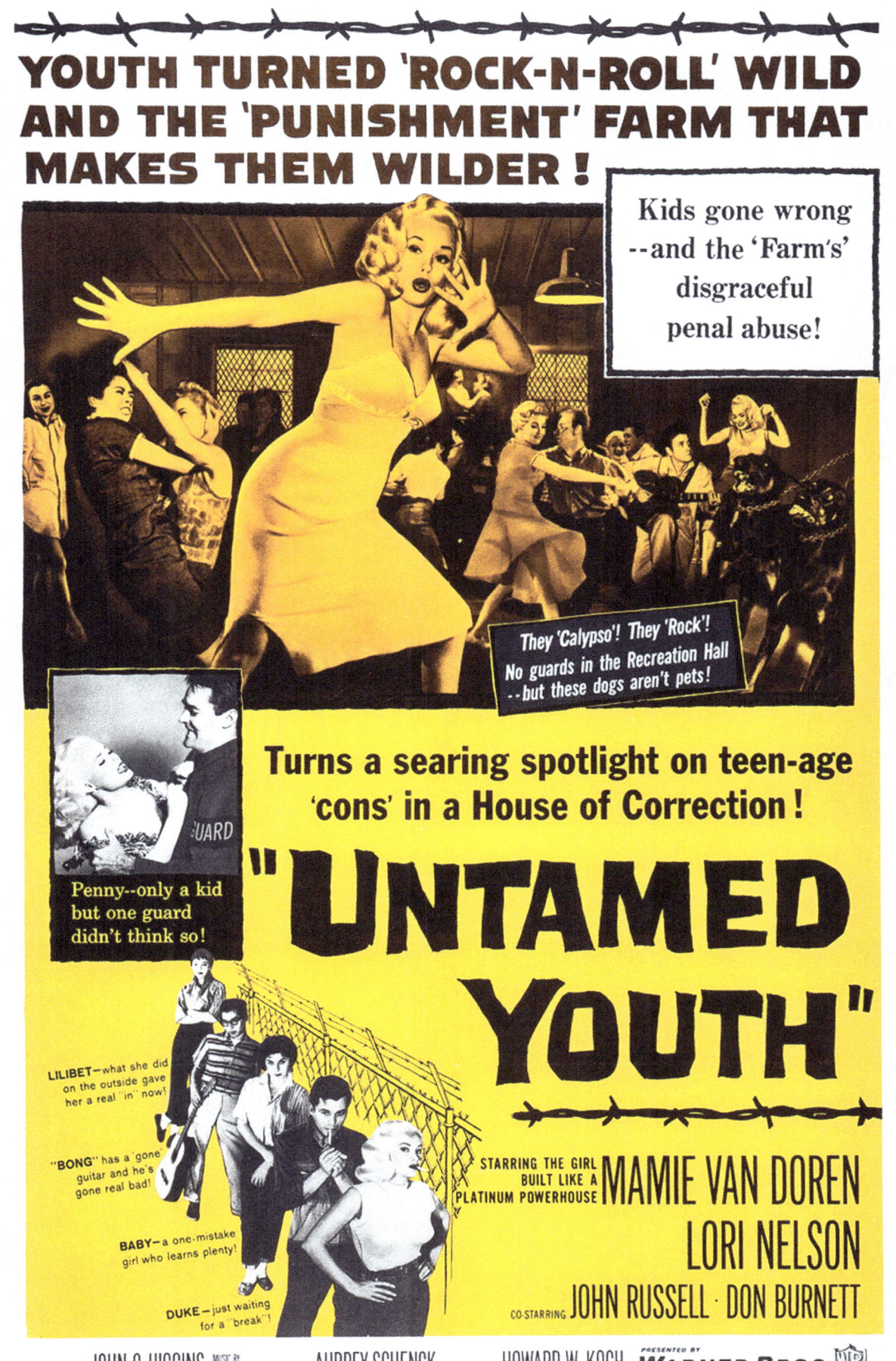

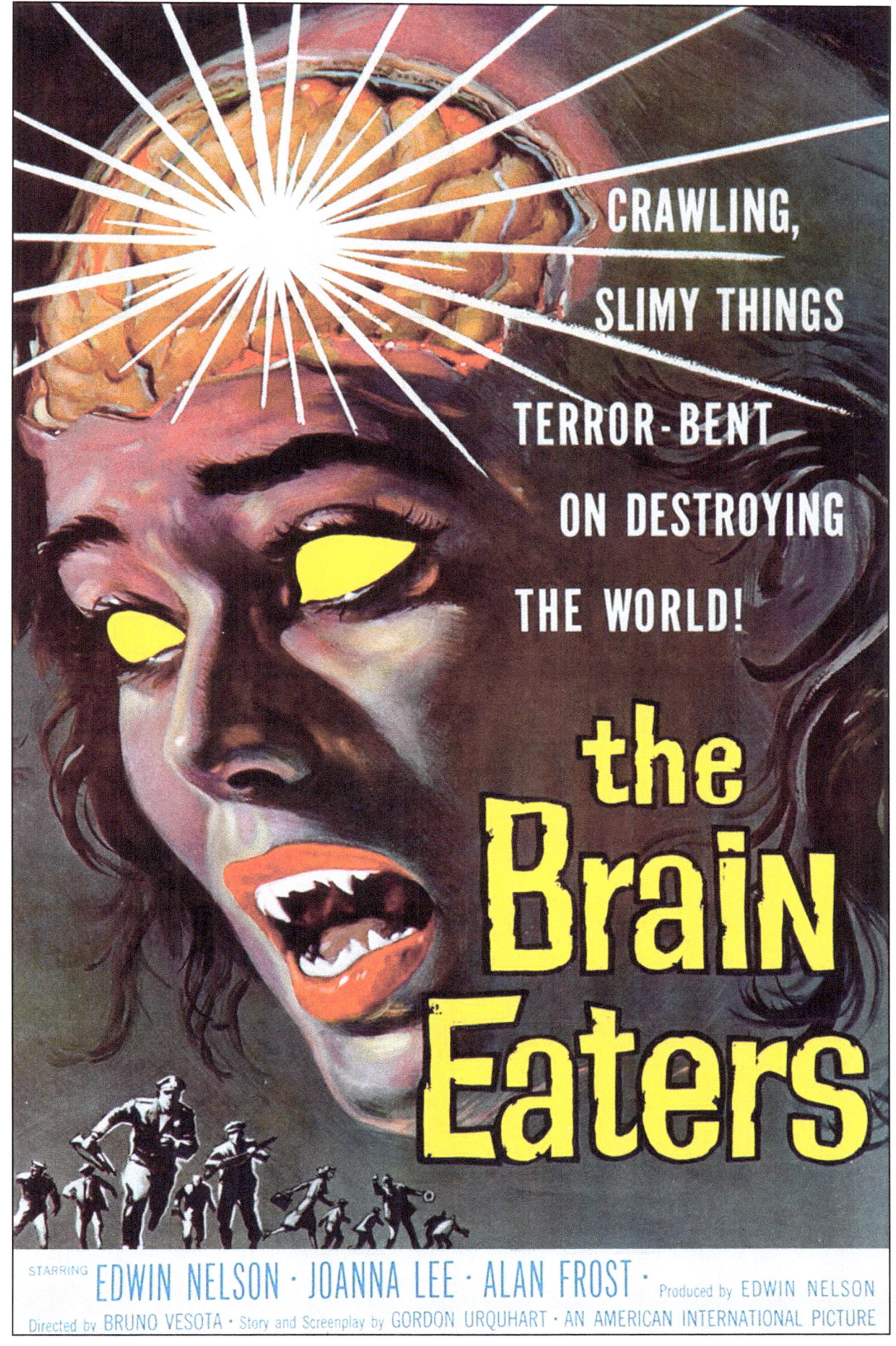

LIKE NOTHING YOU'VE EVER SEEN BEFORE!
METRO-GOLDWYN-MAYER Presents
A KING BROTHERS Production
GORGO
Starring
BILL TRAVERS · WILLIAM SYLVESTER
With
Vincent Winter • Bruce Seton • Joseph O'Conor
Martin Benson • Barry Keegan • Dervis Ward
Christopher Rhodes
Screen Play by JOHN LORING and DANIEL HYATT
Original Story by EUGENE LOURIE and DANIEL HYATT
Directed by EUGENE LOURIE
Produced by FRANK KING and MAURICE KING
TECHNICOLOR

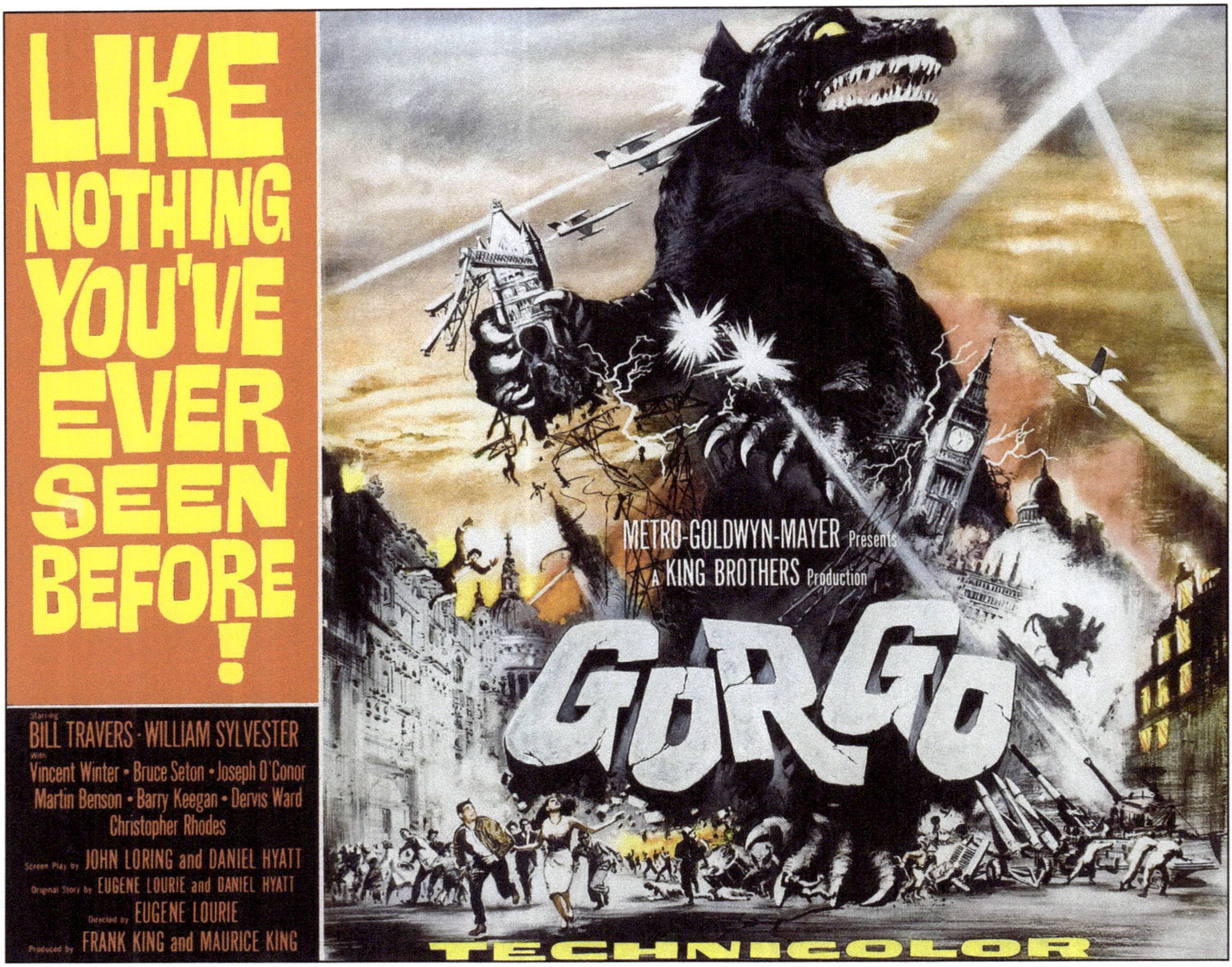

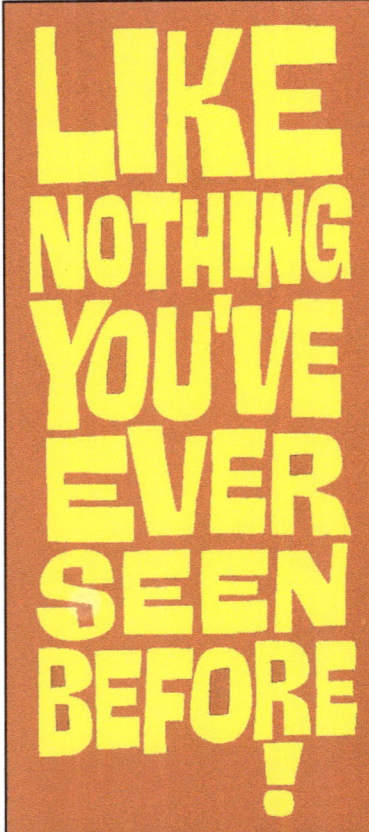

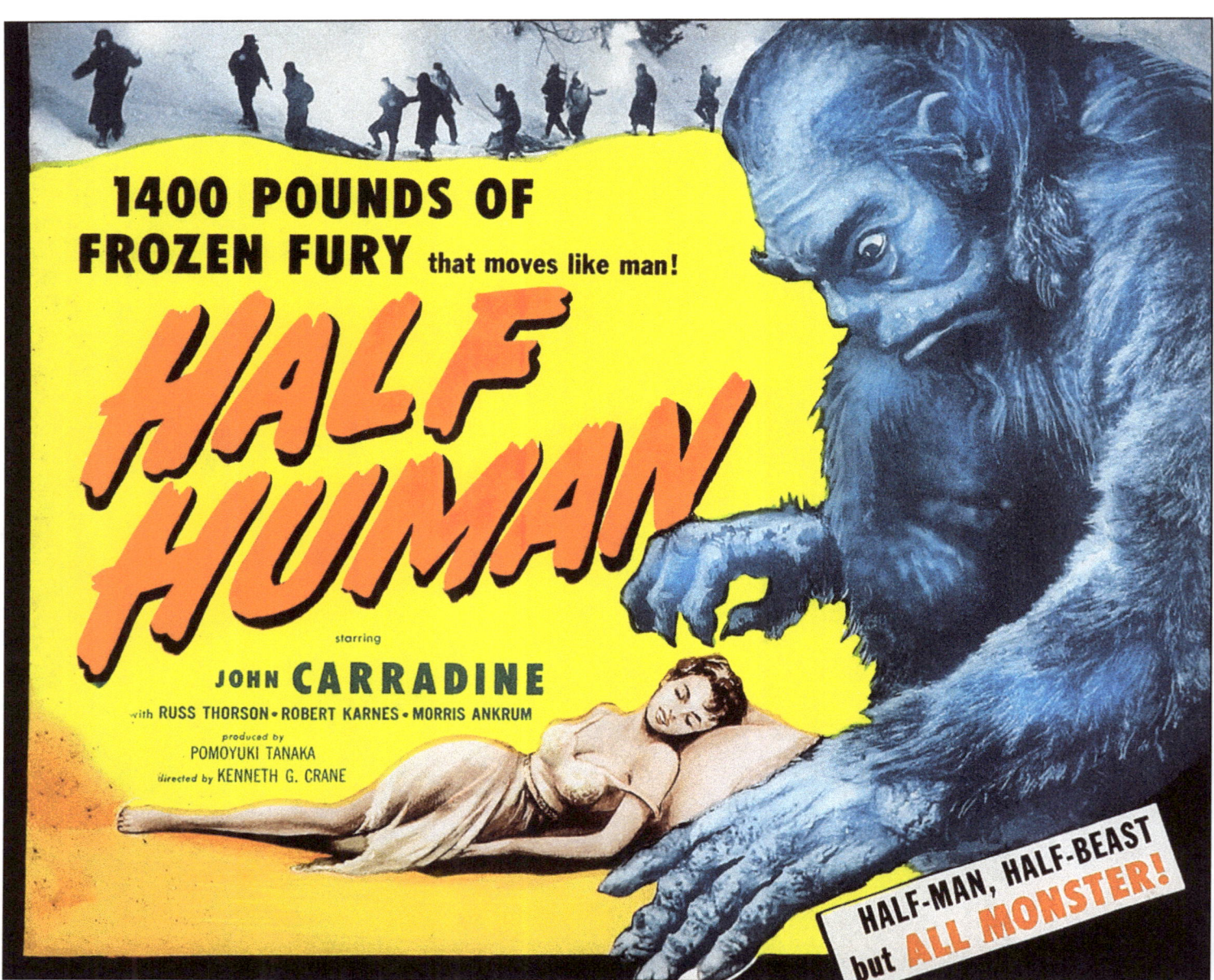

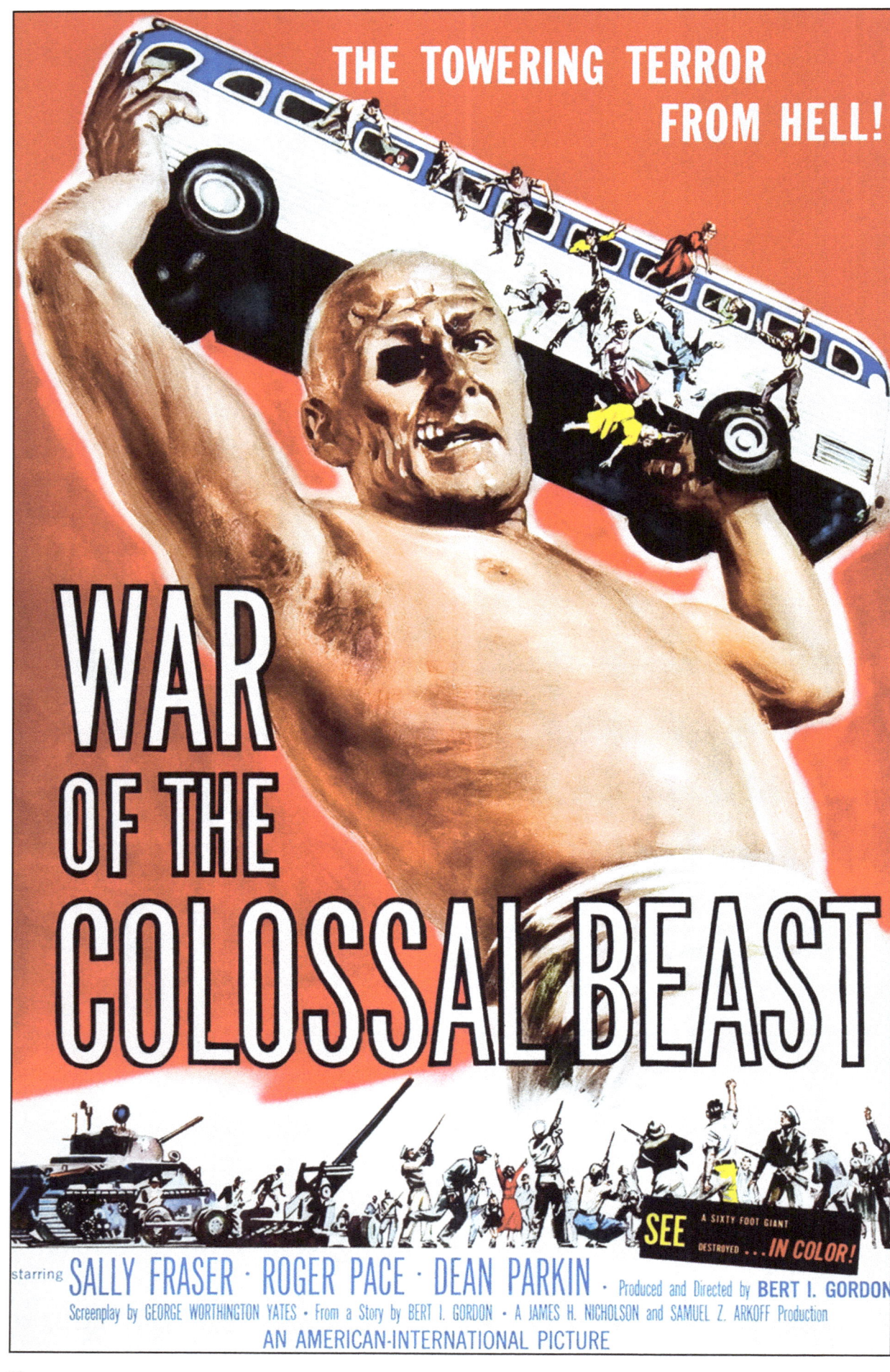

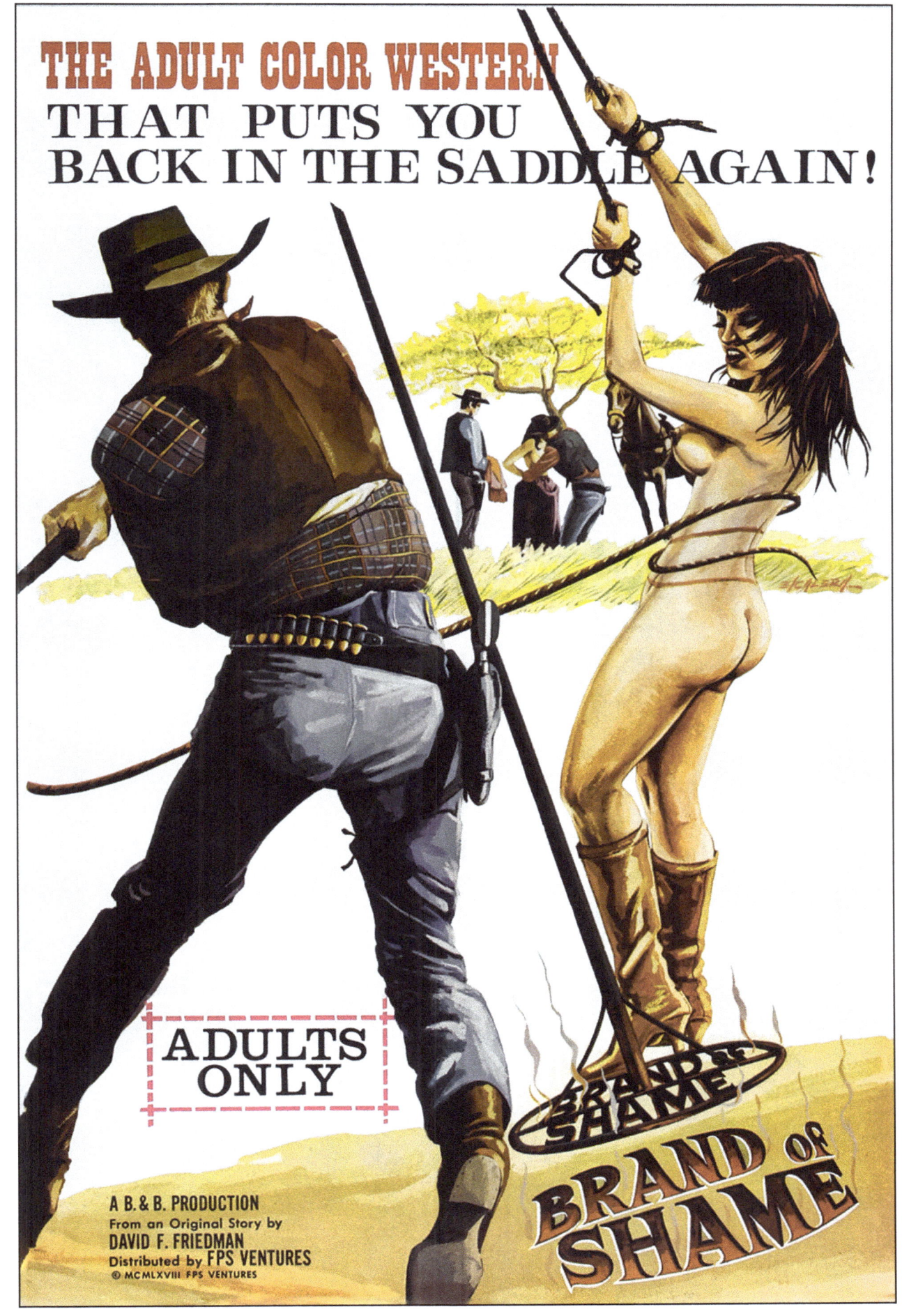

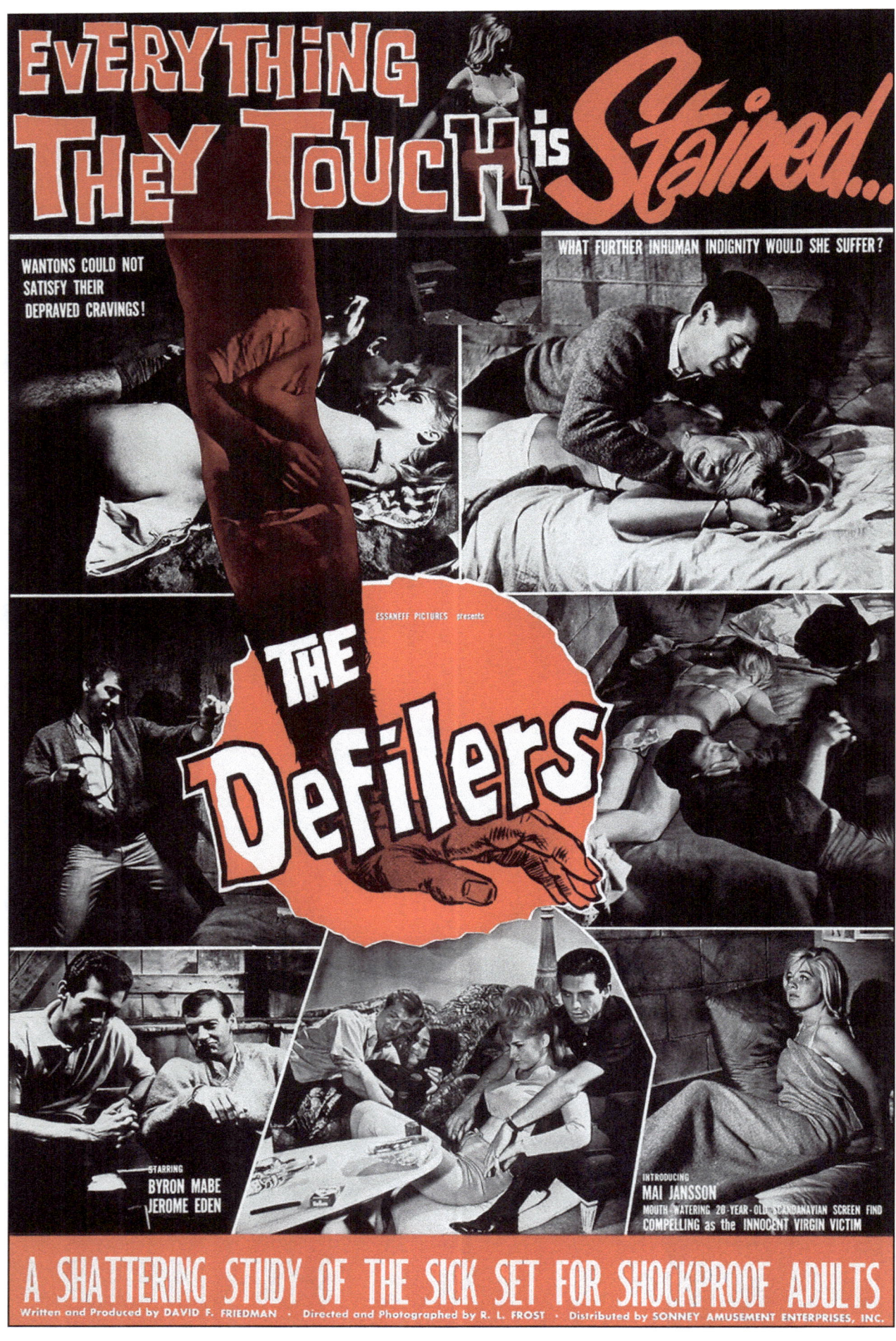

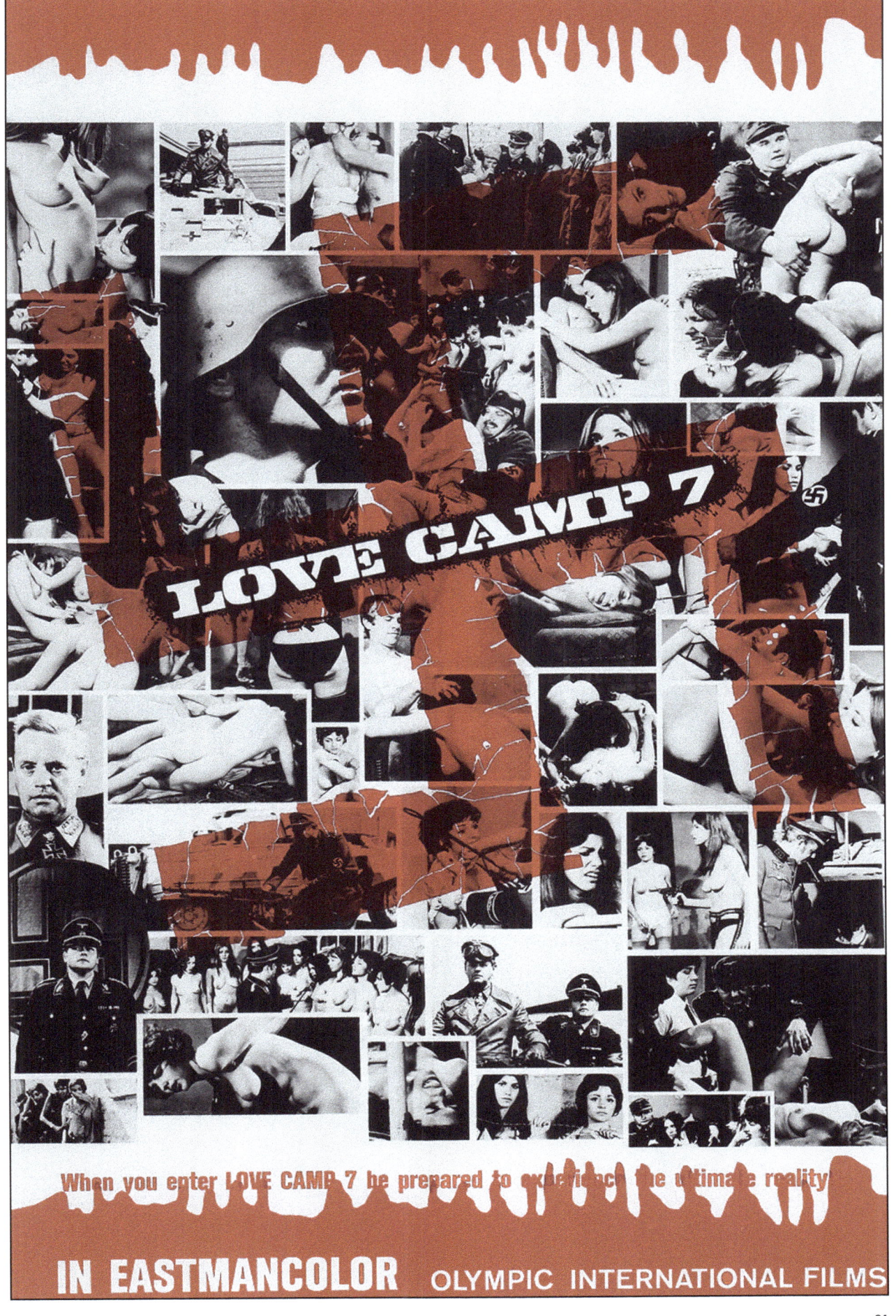

# A MIND-BLOWER!

you may not believe it, but believe it or not... THIS IS...

# Like it is

IN RAW, STARK **COLOR**

"more than just a film... an experience!"

**NEW AND ADULT!**

Directed By WILLIAM ROTSLER
Produced By CHRIS WARFIELD
ORIGINAL MUSIC BY GREG POREE

COPYRIGHT ©1968—A LIMA PRODUCTION

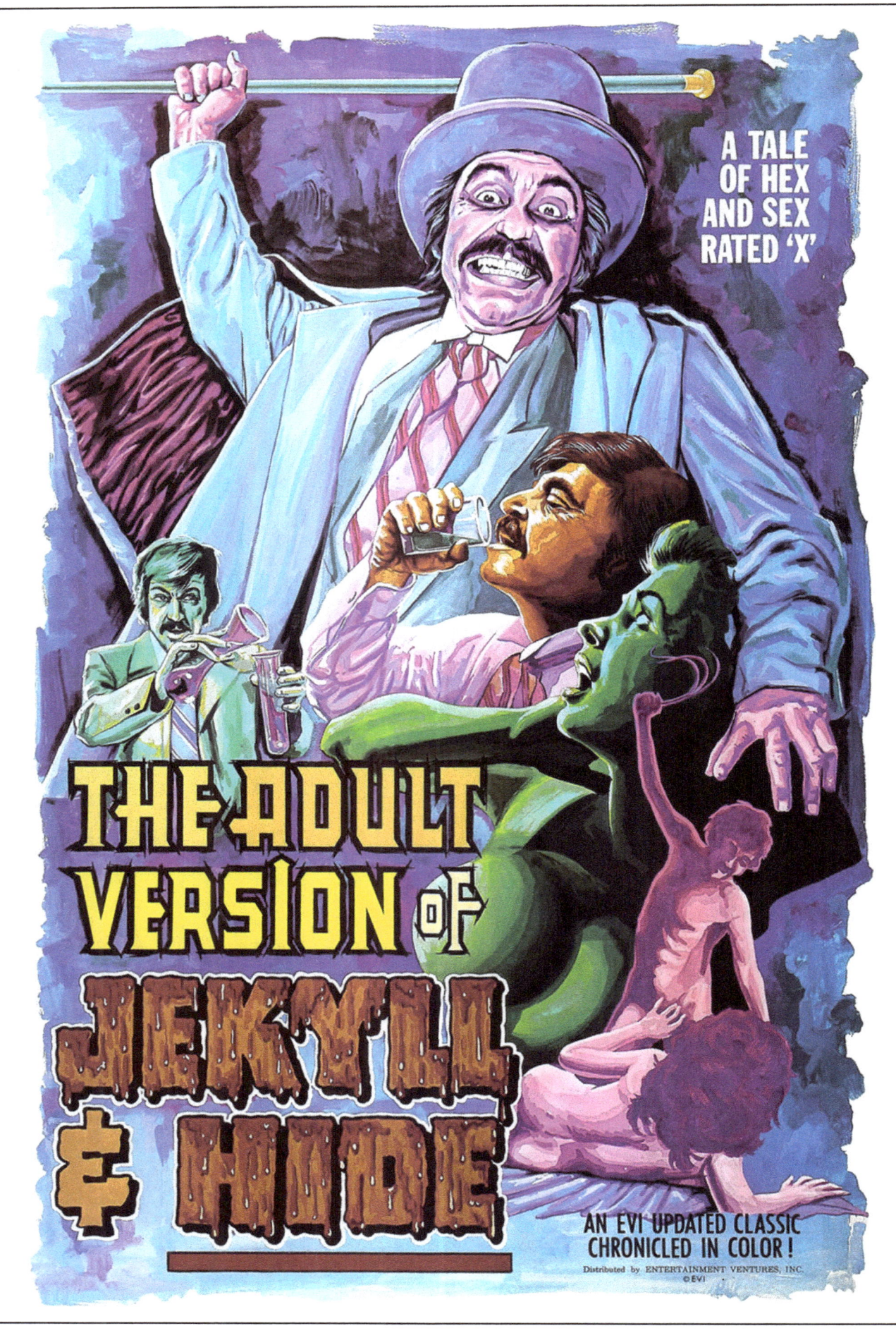

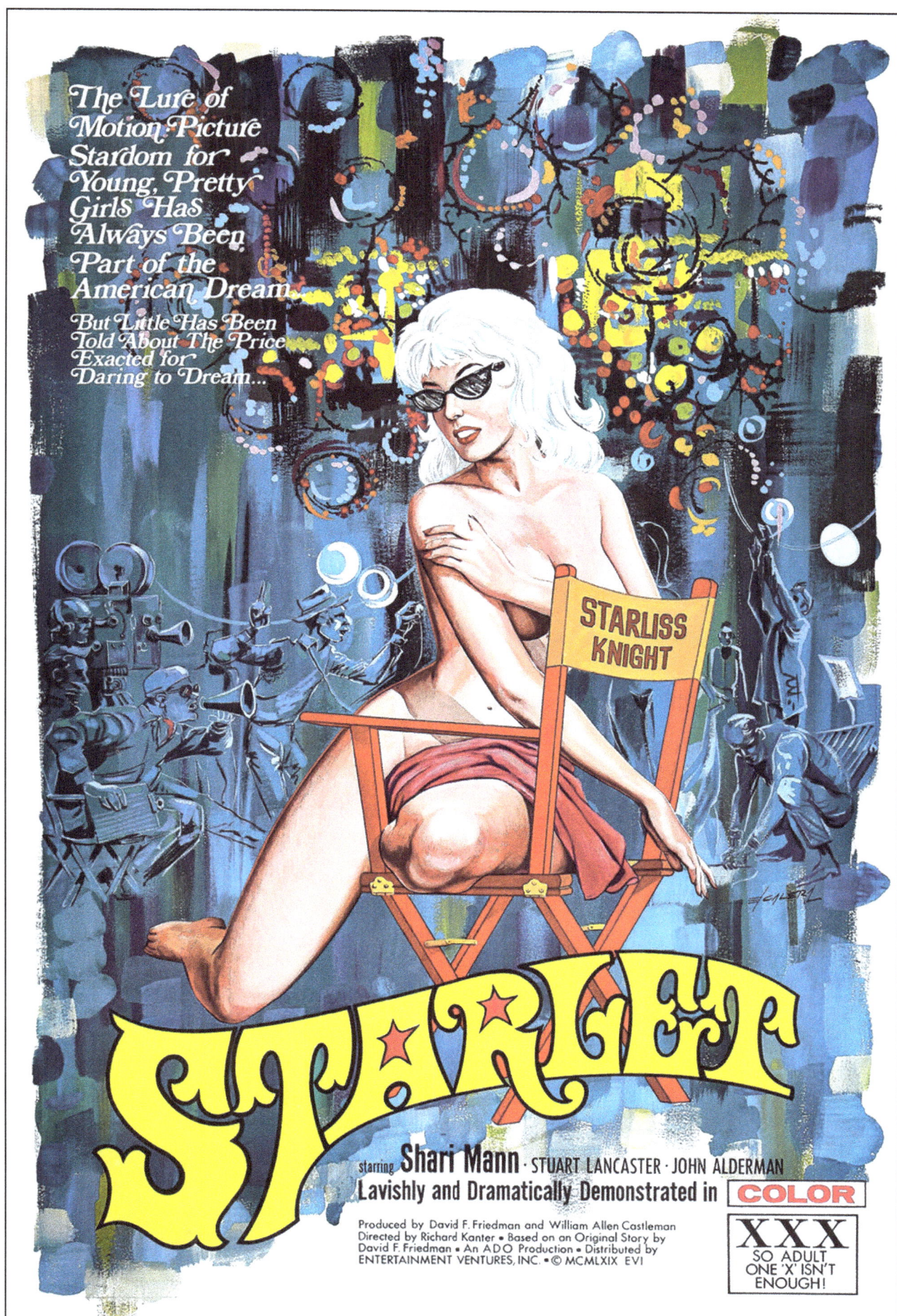

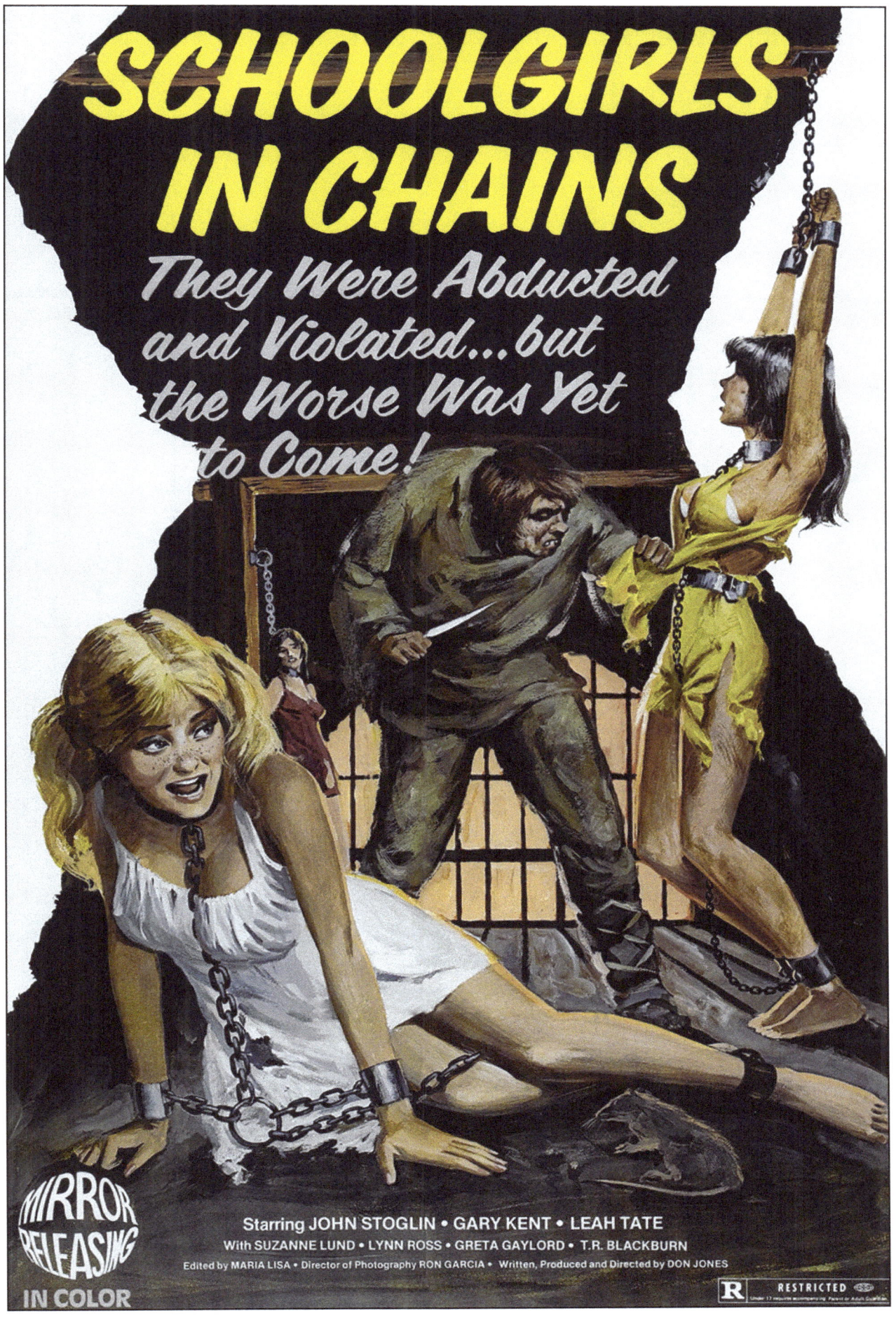

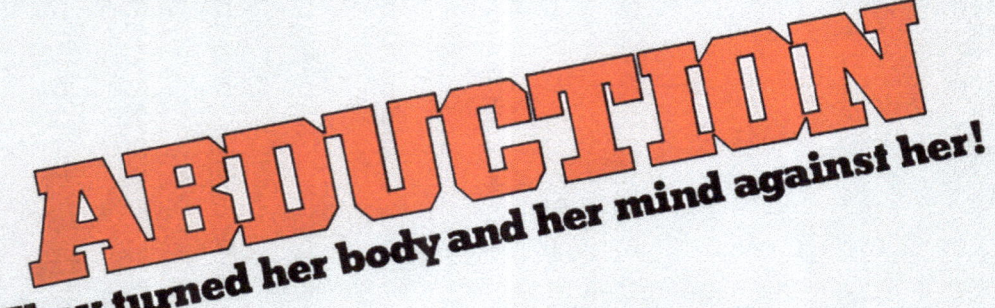

MEET GINGER–
Her weapon is her body...She can cut you, kill you or cure you!
To bust a ring that specializes in assorted sports you need a girl who's played them all!
"GINGER"
ADULTS ONLY
"GINGER" starring CHERI CAFFARO with CINDY BARNETT · MICHELE NORRIS · HERB KERR · WILLIAM GRANNELL · Director of Photograph R. KENT EVANS
Music Composed, Arranged and Conducted by ROBERT G. ORPIN · Produced by RALPH T. DESIDERIO · Written and Directed by DON SCHAIN
A DERIO PRODUCTION Released by JOSEPH BRENNER ASSOCIATES, INC. • COLOR by Deluxe®

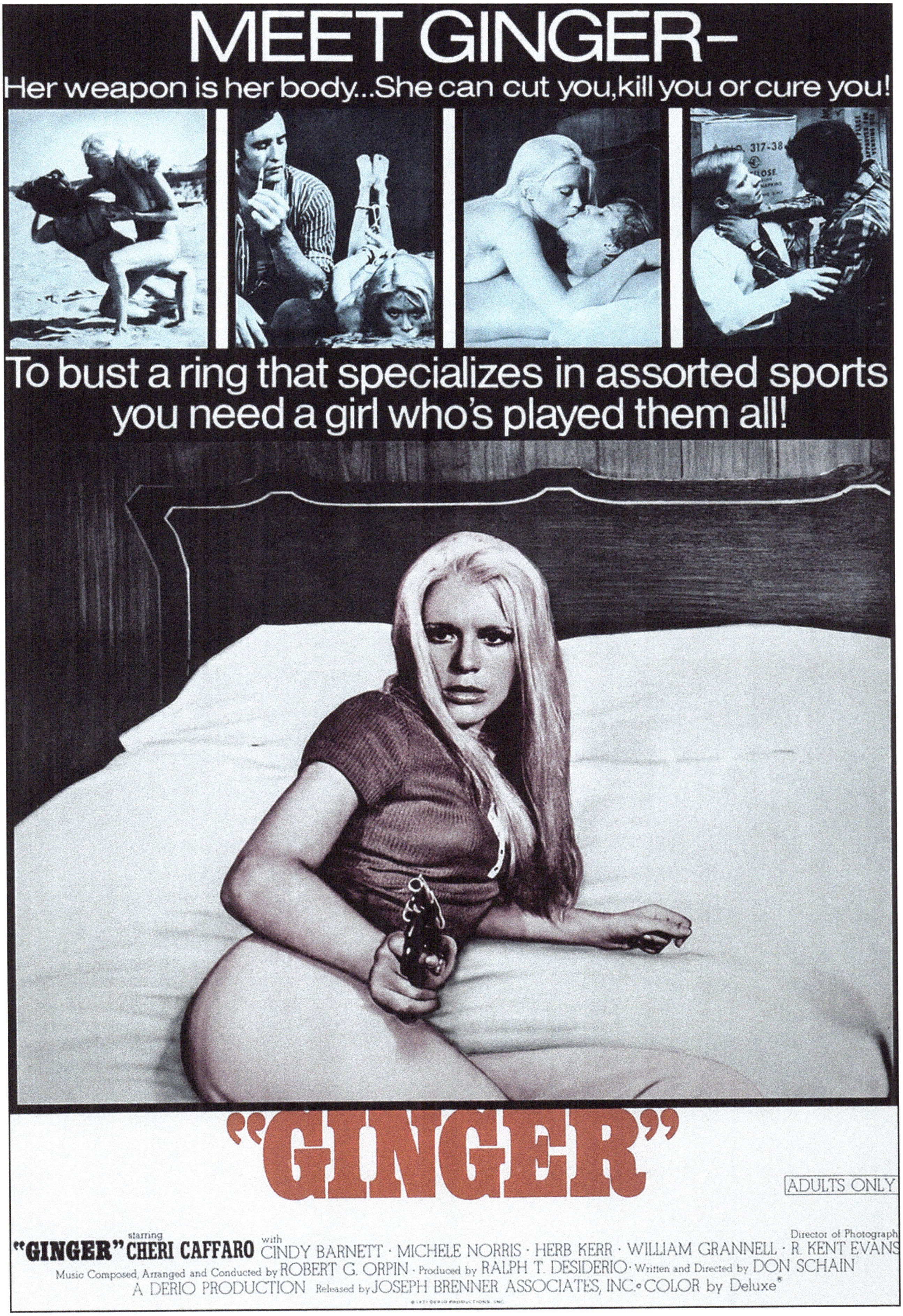

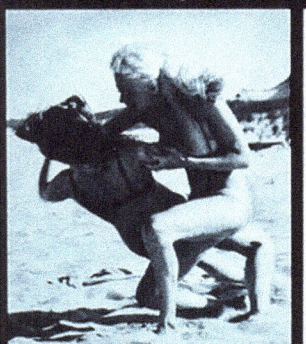

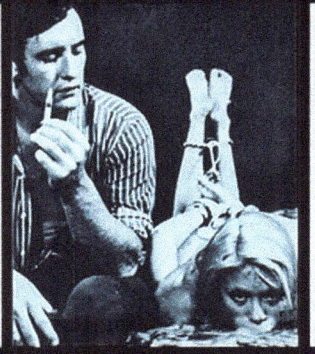

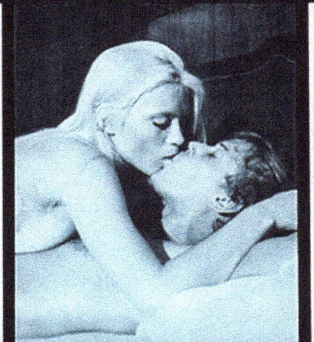

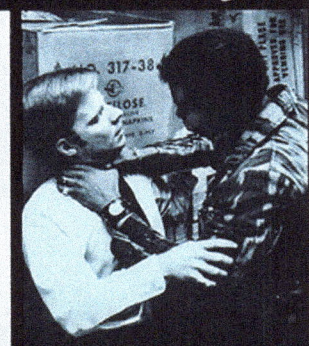

FILM POSTER COLLECTIONS FROM G.H. JANUS

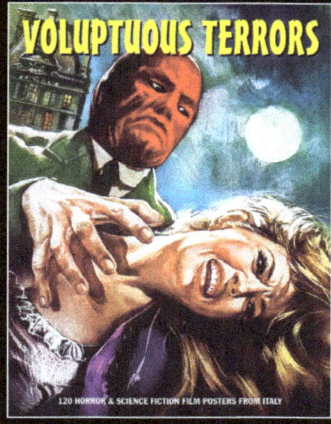

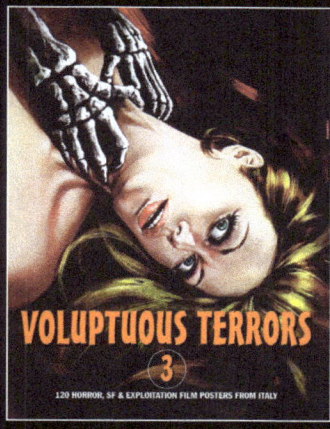

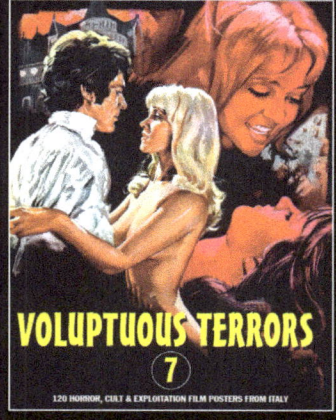
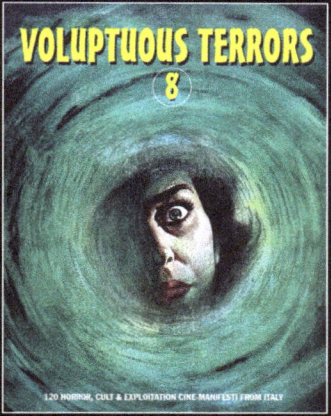

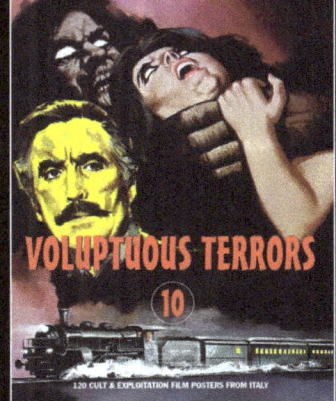
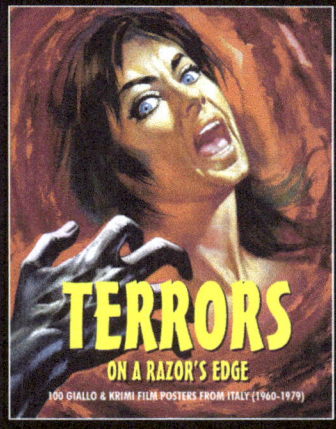
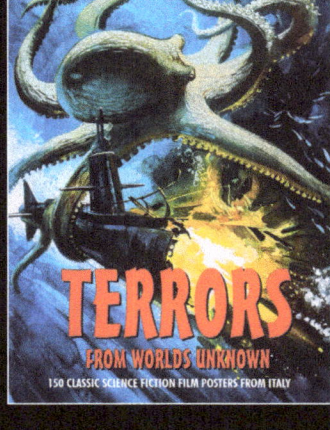

# FILM POSTER COLLECTIONS FROM G.H. JANUS

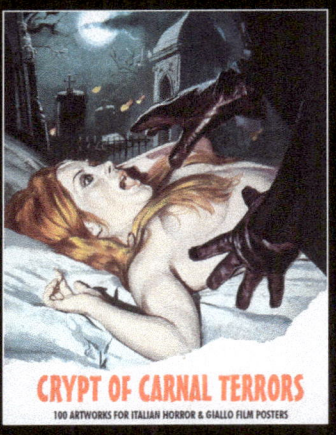
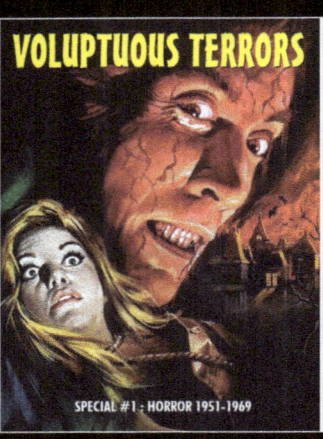

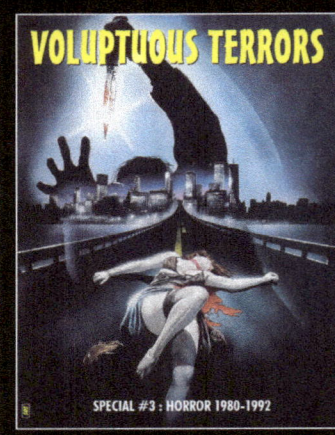
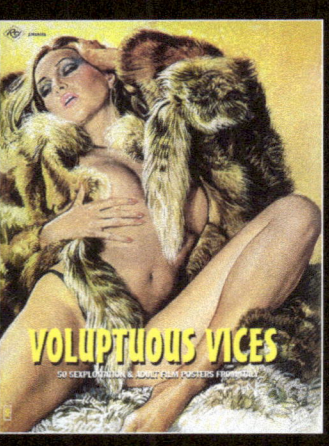

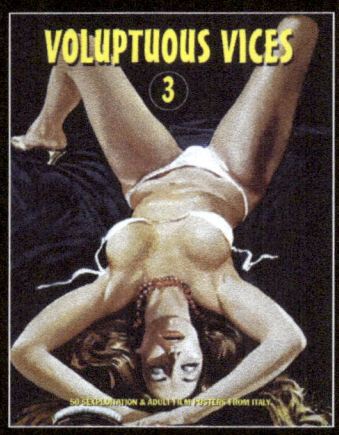
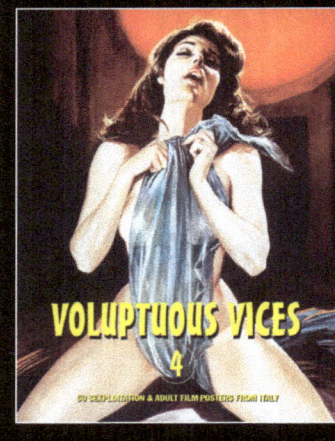
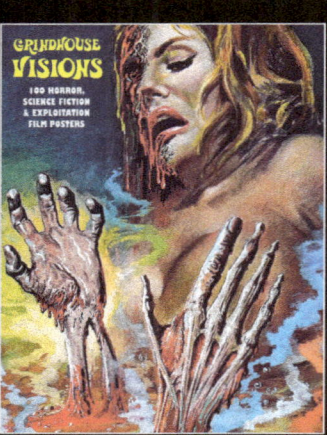
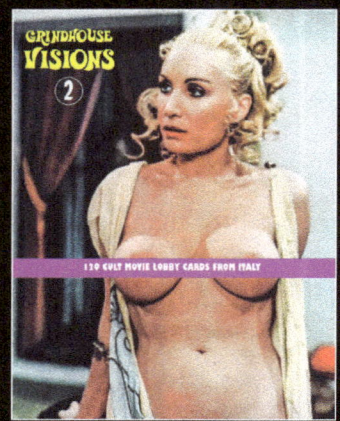
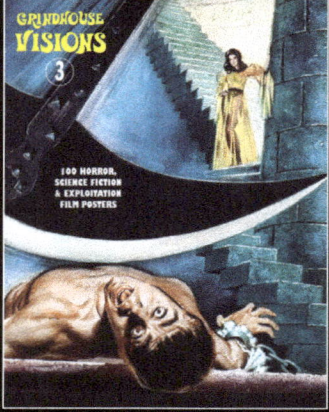

www.ingramcontent.com/pod-product-compliance
Lightning Source LLC
Chambersburg PA
CBHW051317110526
44590CB00031B/4379